" This Book Donated By..."

Tom & Devorah Miller
1998

NORTH-SOUTH BOOKS : NEW YORK

Fly Away, Fly Away Over the Sea

And Other Poems for Children by *Christina Rossetti*

Selected and Illustrated by *Bernadette Watts*

FLY away, fly away over the sea,
  Sun-loving swallow, for summer is done;
Come again, come again, come back to me,
  Bringing the summer and bringing the sun.

When the cows come home the milk is coming,
Honey's made while the bees are humming;
Duck and drake on the rushy lake,
And the deer live in the breezy brake;
And timid, funny, brisk little bunny
Winks his nose and sits all sunny.

IF a mouse could fly,
    Or if a crow could swim,
Or if a sprat could walk and talk,
    I'd like to be like him.

If a mouse could fly,
    He might fly away;
Or if a crow could swim,
    It might turn him grey;
Or if a sprat could walk and talk,
    What would he find to say?

If stars dropped out of heaven,
    And if flowers took their place,
The sky would still look very fair,
    And fair earth's face.

Winged angels might fly down to us
    To pluck the stars,
But we could only long for flowers
    Beyond the cloudy bars.

THE peach tree on the southern wall
    Has basked so long beneath the sun,
Her score of peaches great and small
    Bloom rosy, every one.

A peach for brothers, one for each,
    A peach for you and a peach for me;
But the biggest, rosiest, downiest peach
    For Grandmamma with her tea.

EIGHT o'clock;
The postman's knock!
Five letters for Papa;
  One for Lou,
  And none for you,
And three for dear Mamma.

WRENS and robins in the hedge,
   Wrens and robins here and there;
Building, perching, pecking, fluttering,
   Everywhere!

'Kookoorookoo! kookoorookoo!'
    Crows the cock before the morn;
'Kikirikee! kikirikee!'
    Roses in the east are born.

'Kookoorookoo! kookoorookoo!'
    Early birds begin their singing;
'Kikirikee! kikirikee!'
    The day, the day, the day is springing.

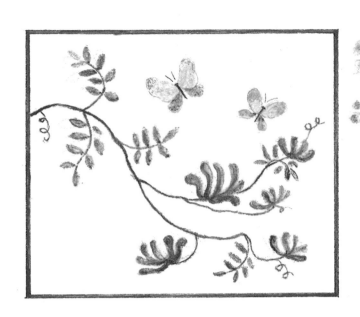

O wind, where have you been,
    That you blow so sweet?
Among the violets
    Which blossom at your feet.

The honeysuckle waits
    For Summer and for heat;
But violets in the chilly Spring
    Make the turf so sweet.

RUSHES in a watery place,
  And reeds in a hollow;
A soaring skylark in the sky,
  A darting swallow;
And where pale blossom used to hang
  Ripe fruit to follow.

O wind, why do you never rest,
    Wandering, whistling to and fro,
Bringing rain out of the west,
    From the dim north bringing snow?

BREAD and milk for breakfast,
    And woollen frocks to wear,
And a crumb for robin redbreast
    On the cold days of the year.

THERE's snow on the fields,
    And cold in the cottage,
While I sit in the chimney nook
    Supping hot pottage.

My clothes are soft and warm,
    Fold upon fold,
But I'm so sorry for the poor
    Out in the cold.

DEAD in the cold, a song-singing thrush,
Dead at the foot of a snowberry bush,—
Weave him a coffin of rush,
Dig him a grave where the soft mosses grow,
Raise him a tombstone of snow.

WHAT are heavy? sea-sand and sorrow:
What are brief? today and tomorrow:
What are frail? Spring blossoms and youth:
What are deep? the ocean and truth.

BOATS sail on the rivers,
   And ships sail on the seas;
But clouds that sail across the sky
   Are prettier far than these.

There are bridges on the rivers,
   As pretty as you please;
But the bow that bridges heaven,
   And overtops the trees,
And builds a road from earth to sky,
   Is prettier far than these.

If all were rain and never sun,
    No bow could span the hill;
If all were sun and never rain,
    There'd be no rainbow still.

Hᴜʀᴛ no living thing:
 Ladybird, nor butterfly,
Nor moth with dusty wing,
 Nor cricket chirping cheerily,
Nor grasshopper so light of leap,
 Nor dancing gnat, nor beetle fat,
Nor harmless worms that creep.

Brown and furry
Caterpillar in a hurry
Take your walk
To the shady leaf, or stalk,
Or what not,
Which may be the chosen spot.
No toad spy you,
Hovering bird of prey pass by you;
Spin and die,
To live again a butterfly.

IF the moon came from heaven,
    Talking all the way,
What could she have to tell us,
    And what could she say?

'I've seen a hundred pretty things,
    And seen a hundred gay;
But only think: I peep by night
    And do not peep by day!'

What do the stars do
    Up in the sky,
Higher than the wind can blow,
    Or the clouds can fly?

Each star in its own glory
    Circles, circles still;
As it was lit to shine and set,
    And do its Maker's will.

THE dog lies in his kennel,
  And Puss purrs on the rug,
And baby perches on my knee
  For me to love and hug.

Pat the dog and stroke the cat,
  Each in its degree;
And cuddle and kiss my baby,
  And baby kiss me.

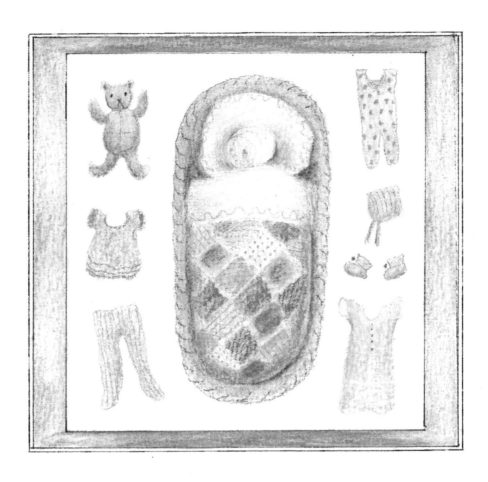

Lullaby, oh lullaby!
Flowers are closed and lambs are sleeping;
    Lullaby, oh lullaby!
Stars are up, the moon is peeping;
    Lullaby, oh lullaby!
While the birds are silence keeping,
    (Lullaby, oh lullaby!)
Sleep, my baby, fall a-sleeping,
    Lullaby, oh lullaby!

All the poems in this collection were taken from *The Poetical Works of Christina Georgina Rossetti*, edited by William Michael Rossetti, published by Macmillan and Company, Ltd., 1904. They were first published in the book *Sing-Song, a Nursery Rhyme Book*, by Christina Rossetti, illustrated by Arthur Hughes, published by George Routledge and Sons, London, 1872.

Farewell

First published in the United States, Great Britain, Canada, Australia and New Zealand in 1991 by North-South Books, New York, an imprint of Nord-Süd Verlag AG, Gossau Zürich, Switzerland.

LIBRARY OF CONGRESS CATALOGING-IN-PUBLICATION DATA
Rossetti, Christina Georgina, 1830–1894.
Fly away, fly away over the sea : and other poems for children / by Christina Rossetti ; selected and illustrated by Bernadette Watts.
"First published in the book Sing-song, a nursery rhyme book, by Christina Rossetti . . . published by George Routledge and Sons, London, 1872."
Summary: Originally published in 1872, many of these poems are now considered childhood classics.
ISBN 1-55858-101-4
1. Children's poetry, English. [1. English poetry—Collections.]
I. Watts, Bernadette, ill. II. Rossetti, Christina Georgina, 1830–1894. Sing-song III. Title.
PR5237.A4 1991
821'.8–dc20 90-42738

BRITISH LIBRARY CATALOGUING IN PUBLICATION DATA
Rossetti, Christina 1830–1894
Fly away, fly away over the sea : and other poems for children.
I. Title II. Watts, Bernadette 1942–
823.8
ISBN 1-55858-101-4

1 3 5 7 9 10 8 6 4 2
Printed in Belgium